PAPER CRAFTS TO MAKE YOU SMILE

Written and Illustrated by Juel Krisvoy

1

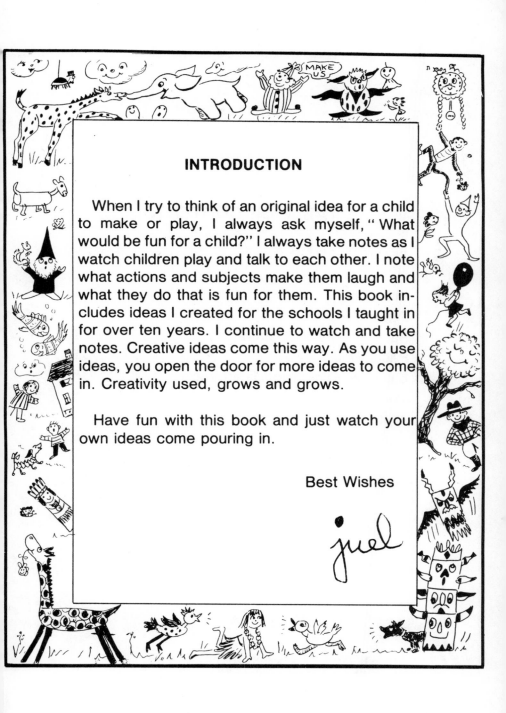

INTRODUCTION

When I try to think of an original idea for a child to make or play, I always ask myself, "What would be fun for a child?" I always take notes as I watch children play and talk to each other. I note what actions and subjects make them laugh and what they do that is fun for them. This book includes ideas I created for the schools I taught in for over ten years. I continue to watch and take notes. Creative ideas come this way. As you use ideas, you open the door for more ideas to come in. Creativity used, grows and grows.

Have fun with this book and just watch your own ideas come pouring in.

Best Wishes

juel

TABLE OF CONTENTS

SECTION TITLES   **PAGES**

PRESCHOOL

VALENTINE MAILBOX

Cut a slit on top of a closed cereal box (to drop in the valentines, when finished). Paint the box a light color and then let it dry.

Draw and cut out a cardboard heart-shaped pattern. Each child then traces some hearts around the pattern onto red construction paper. Draw eyes, noses and mouths on the hearts with a black fine line marker. Cut out the hearts and glue them onto the painted mailbox to receive valentines to take home on Valentine's Day.

EASTER BUNNIES

CEREAL BOX EASTER BUNNY HEAD: Make a cardboard pattern of the Easter Bunny's head and neck. The child traces around the pattern onto stiff white paper. Draw the eyes, nose and mouth, with a black fine line marker. Add the whiskers and cut out the head.

BODY: Measure the height and circumference of the box with a tape measure. (Help the children do this as a learning experience.) Have them measure out the correct size, then cut it out and glue the white paper onto the cereal box. Draw legs with a fine line black marker. Tie a crepe paper ribbon around the bunny's neck. Cut a slit on the top front edge of the box for the bunny's neck to go through. Put glue on the front neck, put the neck through the slit and press it in place. Then glue the box top closed.

NOTE: If you wish to avoid getting glue and paper on the body, you can simplify the method by just painting the cereal box body white with gesso. Glue a cotton ball tail on the back.

EASTER BUNNIES (cont'd.):

TUBE HEAD EASTER BUNNY

HEAD: Take stiff white paper and place a ruler along the bottom edge. Show the child how to mark off 16 inches. He makes a dot on the paper. Then he places the ruler vertically on the paper and makes another dot to show 10 inches for the height. Do this at both ends of the 16-inch width.

Place the ruler at the top of the 10-inch verticals and draw a 16-inch line to join the 10-inch verticals to form a rectangle. Then cut it out. Staple the two vertical ends together to form a *Tube Head*. Now draw a bunny face and whiskers.

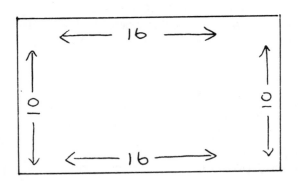

BUNNY EARS: Make a cardboard pattern of an 8-inch-high bunny ear. The child traces two bunny ears onto stiff white paper. Color pink in the centers of the ears; then cut them out. Staple the bottom of the ears inside of the top of the bunny's head.

BOW TIE: Cut out a small rectangle of crepe paper. Twist it in the center and glue or staple it to the bottom of the head (see picture).

HALLOWEEN GHOST

Cut out a piece of white tissue paper 12 inches long by 5 inches wide. Fold the 12-inch length in half. Crumple one white facial tissue inside of the folded tissue paper right under the fold.

Tie a piece of heavy white thread around the ghost's neck to keep the stuffing inside his head and to give the ghost a shape. Draw two eyes and a smile with a black thin line marker. Thread a needle (with a large eye) with heavy thread. Push the needle through the top of the ghost's head. Then remove the needle and tie the two ends of the thread together. Now you can hold the end of the thread as the ghost hangs below to scare people. (Children learn to use needle while they are making this.)

HAPPY HALLOWEEN

A HANGING CHRISTMAS TREE

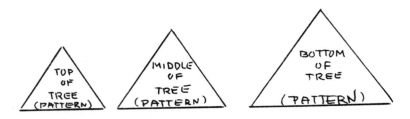

Draw a pattern for three triangles on pieces of cardboard--a smaller triangle, a medium sized triangle and a larger triangle.

Each child traces the three triangles on green heavyweight paper and then cuts them out. The child then glues his medium sized triangle onto the top point of the large triangle; then he glues the small triangle onto the top point of the medium triangle. The tree part is done. Now let each child trim his tree. Cut out and glue on colorful pieces of decorative paper as ornaments. Add a little sparkle fringe used on regular Christmas trees--whatever you like. Staple a red yarn loop at the top to hang up the tree.

MY ZOO

Draw simple zoo animals on cardboard and cut them out as patterns. The children trace around each pattern twice, on stiff paper. Color each animal and cut out the two matching pieces. Put glue on the head and neck of one animal and press it onto its matching piece. Staple the top of the animal's back. Spread the animal's legs apart so that the

animal can stand up. Endless animals can be made this way. Each child can make his own zoo. Have Fun!

HAPPY SUN

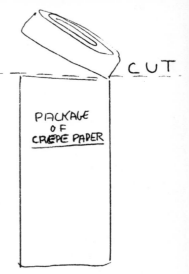

Have each child trace around a plate onto a stiff white piece of paper to make a circle. Cut it out. This will be the sun. Paint it yellow." Draw the eyes, nose and mouth with a fine line black marker. Prepare long strips of orange crepe paper by cutting across the top of a package of orange crepe paper. Help the children to measure a strip of crepe paper that will fit around the outside

edge of the sun. Cut off the right sized strip; then hold the strip with two hands, while the child snips small cuts along the edge to make a long orange fringe. Put glue along the BACK EDGE of the sun and press on the fringe (uncut edge) around it. The fringe will now be framing the sun, representing its rays. Tape a loop of yarn on the top (in back) to hang it by.

8

FRIENDLY INDIAN HEADDRESS

HEADBAND: Each child decorates a strip of paper that is long enough to encircle his head.

FEATHERS: Draw a cardboard feather as a pattern. Have each child trace around the feather and make six feathers. He prints his name near the top of each feather. All children color and cut out their feathers. All of the feathers are put into a paper bag, and each child takes out six feathers from the bag. Help the children to staple the bottom of their feathers to the backs of their headbands. (The prongs of the staple must be on the outside of the headbands to avoid scratching their foreheads.) Each child now wears a friendly Indian headdress or friendly feathers made by friends.

LADYBUG

Each child paints one egg cup (cut out of an empty egg carton) bright red. When the red paint dries, he paints a little black in front by the ladybug's face; then he paints black spots all over the rest of the ladybug. Let the paint dry. Tape the end of a long thread just inside the front of the ladybug, to pull her around or hang her up. (A little mouse can be made this way, too. He would be a different color and could have paper ears and a string tail.)

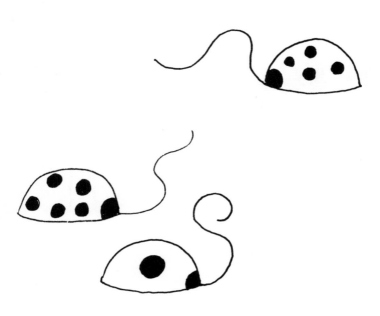

HOUSE: To make the house pattern, draw a cardboard rectangle 9 inches long by 5 inches wide. Each child traces around the pattern onto a piece of construction paper. Fold the 9-inch length of paper in half. This becomes a 4½-inch tall house that is 5 inches wide. Draw the roof by the fold and add the windows, door, etc. Color both sides of the house. Punch a hole in each of the four corners. Stand up

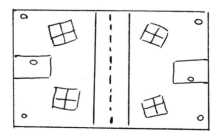

the folded house and push a piece of pipe cleaner through the front and back holes of the left side. Repeat with another piece of pipe cleaner on the right side. Be sure end pieces are hidden inside.

MY HOUSE AND FINGER
PEOPLE (cont'd.):

FINGER PEOPLE: Measure
the length and cir-
cumference of a finger of
the largest child in the
class. Use these
measurements to draw a
small cardboard rectangle.
(Add just a little to the circumference.) The cardboard rectangle is a pattern each child will trace
onto white paper. Cut it out; then encircle the
child's finger with the paper rectangle to form a
tube. Tape at the top of the back seam and
around the bottom of the paper tube. Slip the
tube off the child's finger. With a black fine line
marker, have him draw a face. You can make a
family of them if you have time.

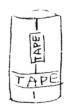

The finger people can live in the house. The children can set
up their houses on a table to make a village and their finger
people can visit back and forth. Stores, schools, etc., can
be made the same way, with necessary variations.

PAPER BAGS

PAPER BAG APARTMENT HOUSE

PEOPLE

CAR

APARTMENT HOUSE
AND PAPER PEOPLE
(WITH SLIP-ON CARS)

APARTMENT HOUSE: Use two paper bags that are the same size. Open up each bag and place one bag inside the other. This will make it a sturdy apartment house that can stand up. The bottom of the bag becomes the roof. The children then draw a door on each side at the open part of the bags. Cut the door so that it opens. Cut on dotted lines (see picture). Glue the double thickness of each door together. Draw as many windows on each side as the child wishes. Color the roof. Now the apartment house can stand up and it is ready to use. Let's make the people.

APARTMENT HOUSE AND PAPER PEOPLE (cont'd.):

PAPER PEOPLE: Draw a simple cardboard pattern for the children to trace around. They trace the patttern on white stiff paper, then color and cut out their people. If they prefer to create their own people, that is even better. The people should be a size that will go through their apartment house doors, so they can walk in and out. Make a stand for the people by stapling a piece of pipe cleaner to the back of each. Turn the end of the pipe cleaner up so it is at a right angle to the paper person. Then twist to form a circle. Now this circle becomes a stand. It also becomes a little handle to move the people about. The children  can make a little city of apartment houses on the floor or on a large table, they can play together with their people going in and out of the apartment houses or they can take them home and show their friends how to make them. Also, the paper people can ride about in slip-on cars.

SLIP-ON CARS: Fold a 4-inch square of construction paper in half. Cut a space on the top fold so you can slip the car right over the head of a paper person. Draw on wheels and doors. The pipe cleaner handle can move him about.

TWO-FACED CLOWN

HEAD AND BODY: Stuff a small paper bag with newspaper for the head; stuff a large paper bag with newspaper for the body. Place the open end of the small bag into the open end of the large bag. Staple them together where they join.

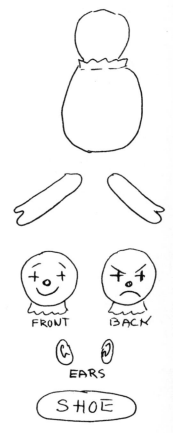

ARMS AND HANDS: Make a cardboard pattern of an arm and hand. Have each child trace two arms and hands onto an extra piece of heavyweight paper bag. Cut them out and staple onto the body. Paint a happy face on one side of the clown head and a sad or angry face on the other side. Staple on ears cut from a piece of paper bag. Paint designs on both sides of the bag to represent a clown suit.

SHOES: Make a large shoe pattern on cardboard. Trace two shoes onto stiff paper. Cut them out and staple them onto the bottom two sides of the bag so they protrude out to the sides, showing as shoes on either side of the clown.

HAT: Cut out a rectangle of paper that will encircle the top of the head. Glue the crepe paper around the top edge of the head and up the back to form a seam. Tie a strip of crepe paper at the top of the hat to bring it to a point.

HAIR: Cut out small squares of orange crepe paper. Cut a fringe on one side of each piece and glue on the back of the clown's ears.

RUFFLE: Cut a long strip of crepe paper (yellow is always good). Glue it around the neck to finish the clown.

NOTE: If you wish to hang up the clown, run a string through two holes made on top of the head before you make the hat. The hat fits over the string which comes out the top to hang it up.

PINATA MONSTER

HEAD AND BODY: Stuff a small paper bag with crumpled newspapers for the head and a large paper bag for the body. Place the open end of the small bag into the open end of the large bag and staple them together to keep the stuffing inside and to form the head and body. Paint a ferocious face on the monster. Paint his body to look fierce and scary.

ADDED PARTS: Be creative! Add any kind of colorful strange ears, arms and hands, wings, or crepe paper hair. Let the children use their imaginations. Put a heavy string through two holes on the head to hang up the pinata monster.

A SCHOOL PARTY: Plan a party. Wrap papers with funny stunts written on the bottom of them around many pieces of candy and put inside before stuffing the body. Hang up the pinata. Blindfold the children and turn them around a few times. With a stick they strike against the pinata monster. When he breaks, all of the candy pours out the bottom.

PINATA MONSTER (cont'd.):

After the children grab for the candy, those who have stunts wrapped around their candy perform one stunt and give their other stunt-wrapped candy to the other children (one for each). Each must perform a stunt.

NOTE: The children who take their monsters home can cut a trapdoor at the bottom, fill it with candy and stunts, and then tape the opening shut. It can then be used for a home birth-day party. If you want to save the pinata, just pull off the trap-door tape and the candy and stunts will still come pouring out. Thus the pinata is protected. Have fun with him.

FUNNY BIRD

BODY: Stuff a large paper bag with newspaper. Close the opening by stapling it. Paint on decorations.

HEAD: Stuff a small paper bag with newspaper. Close the neck opening by stapling it. Then cut a slit on top at the front of the body for the neck of the bird to enter (see arrow in picture). Staple the neck to the body. Paint on the eyes.

BEAK: (one kind) Cut a strip of construction paper with the ends pointed. Fold up on the dotted lines. The X in the center is taped horizontally to the head.

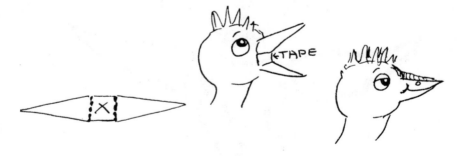

SECOND KIND OF BEAK: Tape the same beak vertically to the head. For this style beak, staple or glue the pointed area together. Use either type beak on your bird.

WINGS, TAIL, AND TOPKNOT: Cut out a square or rectangle of crepe paper, any color and size you choose, for each of these parts. Cut a fringe on the end of each part. Staple them onto the colorful bird as wings, tail and topknot.

LEGS: Cut out of construction paper. Glue them on. Tie a string through two holes cut on top of the head. Tie a second string through two holes cut on top of the body. The strings are used like you would hold a marionette, to walk the bird about. Often a child who is shy will communicate with a puppet or marionette before he will talk to people.

HULA DOLL

BODY: Stuff one large paper bag with crumpled newspapers.

HEAD: Stuff a small paper bag with crumpled newspapers. Place the open end of the small bag into the open end of the large paper bag and staple them together.

ARMS AND HANDS: Cut out two arms and hands from a piece of paper bag and staple them onto the body.

LEGS AND FEET: Cut out two legs with feet from a piece of paper bag and staple onto the body.

HAIR: Cut out a rectangle of black crepe paper long enough to encircle the hair area of the doll's head and wide enough to give her nice long hair. Cut a fringe to make it look like hair and glue on her head. Cut a smaller rectangle and fringe to glue on for bangs.

FACE: Paint on her eyes, nose and mouth or use marker.

HULA SKIRT: Choose the length skirt you wish, then measure the body circumference. Cut out this size as a long crepe paper rectangle. Cut a fringe along the bottom. Glue the top area around the doll's waist.

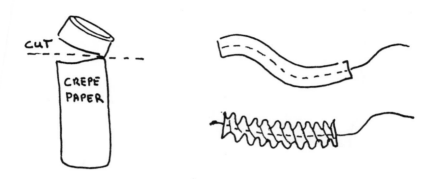

LEI: Cut a strip about 1 ½ inches wide from a package of crepe paper. Unravel the length you want your lei and sew down the center of the crepe paper strip. Pull up the strip as you sew to form a ruffle effect (like flowers).

Add as many strips as you need until the thread is filled with one long ruffle look. Tie the ends of the string together and the lei is ready to wear.

NOTE: This lei is fun for girls to make and wear. Shorter strips of many colors can be used in the long lei ruffle. The boys can make them to give to their mothers or sisters.

BLACK SCOTTISH TERRIER

DOG: Make a cardboard pattern of the dog's head, body and tail. Trace them twice on black construction paper and cut out.

LEGS: Color pipe cleaners black with crayon. Fold them in half and turn up their toes into small loops.

BODY: Staple the top of the dog's back pieces together. Then tape the tops of the two pairs of legs inside of the body. Glue the head and tail pieces together.

BOW: Cut out a colorful strip of crepe paper to tie around the dog's neck.

EYES: Glue on two tiny dots of paper or two sequins.

NOTE: A more complete dog can be made by glueing on black crepe paper fur. Cut out small strips of crepe paper and cut a fringe along the bottom of each strip. Glue strips onto the dog, starting at the stomach and continuing up to his back. The pieces should overlap a little to look like fur.

MONKEY

INSIDE OF MONKEY: Take a pipe cleaner and twist a loop at the top for the head and turn up the other end as the tail.

ARMS: Twist another pipe cleaner around the body pipe cleaner to become the base to make the arms. Turn up the ends to become hands. (See diagrams below.)

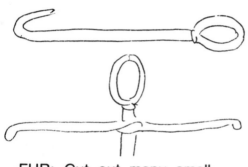

LEGS AND FEET: Twist another pipe cleaner around the lower part of the body pipe cleaner to be the base for the legs and feet. (See below.)

FUR: Cut out many small strips of crepe paper and cut small fringes on one edge of each strip. Glue strips all over the pipe cleaner arms, body, legs and tail.

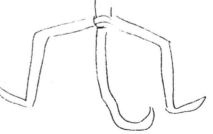

HEAD: Draw a face on yellow constructon paper, cut out, glue in place, and glue crepe paper hair on the back.

SWEATER: Glue colorful crepe paper around the body. Note: Monkey can be twisted into different shapes.

26

MR. SPIDER

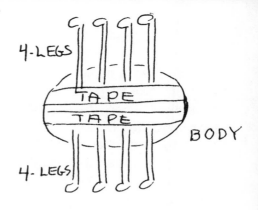

BODY: Cut out a construction paper oval. Color it to look like a suit. On the opposite side of the oval, lay 4 pipe cleaners that have been colored black and have had the ends turned up as spider feet. Tape across the pipe cleaners to hold them in place. Fold this spider body oval in half across the center of the legs.

HEAD: Make a cardboard pattern and trace it twice. Draw hat and face and cut them out. Glue head and hat pieces together. Make a slit on top of body for the neck to slip inside. Staple it in place.

Tie a thread through a small hole on the top of the spider's back to hold him or hang him up.

ELF

BODY: Fold a pipe cleaner in half, twisting the ends together. Then twist the loop top to become the base for the head. ARMS: Run a pipe cleaner through the body loop. Twist the pipe cleaner around the body sides and fold over the extra pieces on the ends as hands. LEGS: Fold a pipe cleaner in half and twist it around the bottom loop of the body. Turn up the feet and fold over the end pieces. (See diagrams below.) ELF SUIT: Cut strips of green crepe paper and twist them around and around the legs, body and arms. Put a little glue here and there. A facial tissue can be held around the body as you cover it with crepe paper strips to give it dimension. HEAD: Draw the Elf's head and face on pink construction paper. Cut out and glue onto pipe cleaner top. Glue orange crepe paper hair on back.

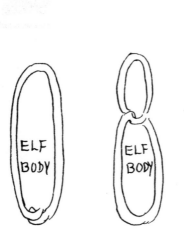

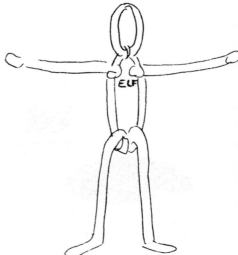

BIRD IN A CAGE

THE CAGE: Cut two squares or rectangles of cardboard. Cut out two pieces of crepe paper the size of the two pieces of cardboard and glue to the cardboard. Make a hole in the four corners of each cardboard piece. Put a pipe cleaner end through the top corner of one cardboard and fold the end over. Then put the other end through the same corner of the bottom cardboard piece and fold it over. One cage bar is now completed. Repeat this by fastening a pipe cleaner bar in each of the remaining three corners. The basic cage is completed, but to make it more like a cage you can add other bars in between the basic four bars.

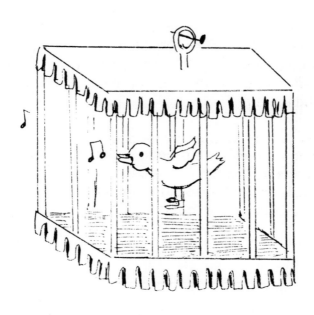

BIRD IN A CAGE (cont'd.):

THE BIRD IN THE CAGE: Draw two identical birds on construction paper and cut them out. Put glue on both birds, except on the wings. Lay the bottom of one pipe cleaner vertically on the glued body of one bird then place the other glued bird on top of the pipe cleaner and press the bird pieces together to hold the pipe cleaner. Bend the unglued wings out on each side. Make a hole in the center of the top of the cage and push the top of the pipe cleaner through it so the bird appears to be hanging or swinging inside the cage. Bend the pipe cleaner on each side of the cage roof so the pipe cleaner will stay in place. Form a loop out of the top of the pipe cleaner outside the top of the cage to hang it up.

FRINGES: A long strip of crepe paper with a fringe cut along the bottom can be glued around the top of the cage to make it more colorful. Also glue another long fringe around the bottom of the cage.

PAPER PLATES

NAME

CUCKOO CLOCK

CLOCK: Make a cardboard pattern by cutting off the rim of a cardboard paper plate. Trace and cut around it on light colored construction paper. Draw on the eyes, mouth, and a dot for the nose. Glue the face to the plate. Make a small hole through the nose for a brass paper fastener. Draw the numbers on the clock with a fine tip black marker.

FASTENER

THE HANDS: Cut out the two clock hands from black construction paper. Make a small hole in the end of each hand and then push the points of the fastener through the holes and the clock's nose. Bend the fastener prongs in back to hold the hands in place.

RUFFLE TO FRAME THE CLOCK: Cut a strip of crepe paper long enough to encircle the outside of the clock. Glue it in place around the rim of the paper plate.

PENDULUM OF CLOCK: Cut out an oval of construction paper and staple it to a strip of construction paper. The child prints his name on the oval. Staple it to the bottom of the clock.

CUCKOO CLOCK (cont'd.):

CLOCK CHAINS: Make two construction paper chains and staple them to the bottom of the clock on either side of the pendulum.

CUCKOO BIRD: Cut out two identical construction paper cuckoo birds. Glue together on the end of a pipe cleaner (leaving the pipe cleaner inside the bird). Do not glue the wings together. Pull them out to each side. Turn up the back end of the pipe cleaner and staple it to the top of the clock. Hang up the clock by stapling a loop of yarn on the back.

Note: This project can be done in simple stages with the children completing a small portion each day. During my many years of teaching, this has always been my "pet" project.

DUCK

BODY: Paint the back of one paper plate yellow. Let it dry. Fold the plate in half.

HEAD: Cut the rim off of another paper plate and use the remaining center part for the head. Paint both sides yellow to match the body.. Paint a black dot on each side for eyes.

THE NECK: Cut from the leftover rim of the plate and paint yellow on both sides. Cut a slit on top of the body for the neck to fit into. Staple it in place. The neck is also stapled to the head.

BEAK: Cut out an orange construction paper beak and glue or staple onto the duck's head. Make a black dot on each side for the duck to breathe.

BEAK

LEGS AND FEET: Use more of the remaining rim of the plate to cut out legs and separate feet. Paint them orange on both sides. Staple the legs to opposite sides of the duck's body.

WINGS AND TAIL: Cut out rectangles of yellow crepe paper all the same size. Then cut a fringe on the end pieces to represent feathers. Staple or glue them onto their proper places.

WINGS AND TAIL

SQUIRREL

BODY AND HEAD: Make a pattern for the head and body that will fit inside a paper plate. Trace this pattern onto the flat areas of two paper plates (don't use the rims). The two matching body and head pieces are then painted brown. Staple the bodies together except at the legs. Glue the head pieces together and staple onto the body. Glue brown crepe paper with a fringe cut along the edge as fur onto the tail. Cut out a strip of white paper to glue around the neck as a collar. Then glue on paper eyes and a crepe paper bow. Spread the legs to stand the squirrel up.

BOW

LIGHTHOUSE AND SAILBOAT

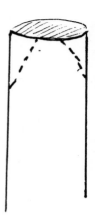

LIGHTHOUSE: Take one cardboard tube. Cut off the top corners and staple the top together. Paint the roof any color you choose. Paint or draw on the windows and railing.

WATER: Paint the inside of a paper plate blue and let it dry. Cut a hole in the center of the plate a little smaller than the bottom of the lighthouse. Tape the bottom of the lighthouse firmly to the bottom of the plate.

SAILBOAT: Make a cardboard pattern for the sailboat as shown. Trace onto stiff white paper, color and cut out. Fold it up on the dotted lines. Glue the sail pieces together. Now you can play.

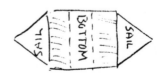

PAPER PLATE DOLL

BODY: Staple two paper plates together to make the body. Paint both sides.

HEAD: Staple two small paper plates together and paint them a light pink flesh color. Paint on the eyes, nose, and mouth. The doll's hair is a rectangle of crepe paper that will encircle the back and sides of her head. Cut a fringe at the bottom to look like hair. Glue in place. You may also add bangs which are smaller but cut out the same way and glued over the forehead.

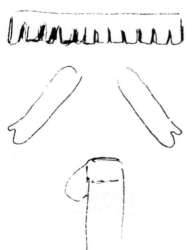

ARMS AND HANDS: Cut out two arm-length rectangles of crepe paper. Glue the sides of each to form two tubes. Hands are two mitten shapes cut out of pink construction paper and stapled to the end of each sleeve. Stuff arms with facial tissues and staple.

THE LEGS: Make two crepe paper tubes. Finish as you did the arms. Staple backs of heels to turn up toes. Glue on paper shoe strips and staple onto both legs. Your doll is ready to play.

Note: A crepe paper strip can be glued around the waist as a skirt.

EASY TWO-DIMENSIONAL PICTURES

Make a sample of each of the five pictures in this section. A child sees how a picture is done and draws it, then he/she has a springboard to create endless versions of his/her own. PATTERNS or freehand can be used. Here are a few examples.

 CHILD WITH A BALLOON: Make a cardboard pattern of a child and a separate pattern of a balloon. Trace the child and balloon on separate pieces of paper. Cut out the balloon.

Color the child and the balloon. Tape or staple the end of a pipe cleaner on the back of the balloon to use as the string. Cut a small hole by the child's hand and push the end of the pipe cleaner through the front. Tape it in place on the back of the picture. Now you have a picture of a child holding a balloon that stands out.

CHILD WITH AN UMBRELLA:

Make a cardboard pattern of a child with a RAINCOAT AND HAT and an open umbrella without a handle. Trace umbrella onto a piece of paper, color and cut out. Trace pattern of child onto another paper. Color child and draw an umbrella handle. Draw and color the picture's background. Cut a small hole by child's hand and push one end of a pipe cleaner through hole. Tape it on back. Tape umbrella in front to top of pipe cleaner. The picture is finished with the umbrella protruding slightly from the picture.

A BOUNCING KITTY:

Make a cardboard pattern of a cat's head. Trace and color the head on a separate piece of paper. Cut it out. Then wind part of a pipe cleaner around your thumb to make a coil effect, leaving the rest of it straight. Tape the end of coil on the back of head. Make a pattern of a cat's neck and shoulders, trace it onto a separate paper, and color it. Cut a small hole in the neck at the X. (See next page.)

A BOUNCING KITTY (cont'd.):

Push the straight end of the pipe cleaner through neckhole, bend it down in back and tape it to back of paper. Glue on a strip of crepe paper as a ribbon and bow. The cat's head protrudes and wiggles.

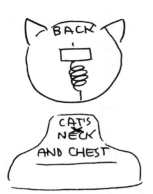

A FRIENDLY TREE:

Make a cardboard pattern of a TREETOP. Trace it onto a piece of paper. Draw a happy smile. Color and cut it out. Wind a pipe cleaner around your thumb, making part of it into a coil shape, the rest of it straight. Tape end of coil on back of treetop. Make cardboard pattern of a TREE TRUNK. Trace it on paper, then draw and color the scenery. Make a hole on top of the tree trunk. Push straight end of pipe cleaner through hole, bend it down in back and tape it to back of paper. The picture is completed.

SAILBOAT:

Make cardboard pattern of two SAILS as one piece. Make a second cardboard

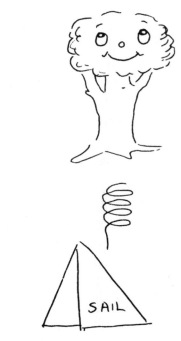

SAILBOAT (cont'd.):

pattern of a boat. Trace the sails onto a piece of paper, color and cut out. Trace the boat onto another paper; draw waves, sky, sea gulls and color. Staple a pipe cleaner in front between the sails. Bend back the bottom of pipe cleaner, so the sails stand out from picture. Make a small hole on top of boat to push part of bent pipe cleaner through, then bend the end down flat against back of picture. Tape it securely.

Note: Cardboard patterns can be used for learning.

Make a box full of cardboard patterns of animals, birds, tops of flowers, butterflies, fish, people, cars, boats, planes, etc. Children learn the basic shapes of things they see by tracing with pencils and coloring them. Soon they start to draw without patterns. Also have a box of mounted patterns and designs from materials, wallpapers, etc., to study and learn color combinations and designs. Children should try to sketch anything they see as artists do. Soon they create things better on their own.

MILK CARTONS

MILK CARTON INDIAN

BODY: A one-quart milk carton will be the body and will hold the head.

HEAD: Cut out an 8 by 4-inch piece of paper to make a 4-inch square by folding it in half. Draw a face and hair. Color; also color hair on the back. Place head on top of milk carton and staple to cover both sides. Put two facial tissues inside head as stuffing. Glue the sides of the head together.

COSTUME: Decorate a piece of paper with INDIAN DESIGNS and glue around the milk carton. If you prefer, use crepe paper. **ARMS:** Cut out a piece of paper 1½ by 9 inches long. Draw a circle in the center as folded hands. Color and draw fingers. Color sleeves to match the costume. Glue X ends of arms, one on each side of body. (They should protrude a little.) **FEATHERS:** Color and cut out paper feathers to glue across top of head.

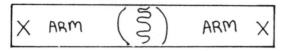

X   ARM   (⌇)   ARM   X

HEADBAND: Decorate a strip of paper to encircle head. Glue it over the bottom of feathers.

TOTEM POLE

Use two empty half-gallon milk cartons. Completely open top of one carton, turn the other milk carton over and push its closed top down into open top of first milk carton. Tape cartons together. Cover BACK of milk cartons with broad strips of crepe paper with a fringe cut on each bottom edge. Glue them, one above the other, starting at the bottom. TOTEM POLE HAS 4 HEADS. Each head is a half of a piece of construction paper 4½ inches by 12 inches. Draw a different 4½-inch-high head on the center of each piece. Glue the heads to the front and sides, one above the other. Glue a strip of crepe paper with a fringe around the top of the head with fringe upward.

HORNS COME OUT OF SIDES.

THEY ARE GLUED ONTO CARDBOARD STRIPS THAT

GO THROUGH A SLIT ON ONE SIDE AND COME

THROUGH AND OUT A SLIT ON THE OPPOSITE SIDE —

HOUSE WITH A "ME" DOLL TO PLAY A HIDING GAME

THE HOUSE: Cut out a 9 by 12-inch piece of construction paper. Cut out most of the back of an empty half-gallon milk carton. Then glue the construction paper onto the front and two sides of the milk carton. Draw the windows and door with a black marker.

ROOF: Cut out a 4 by 7-inch piece of construction paper. Fold the 7-inch length in half. Place the fold of the roof over the top of milk carton, which has been stapled shut. Staple top of roof to top of milk carton. Make a roof design with a black marker. Now you need a "ME" DOLL in the house. Draw and cut out a small paper doll that looks like you. Tape a pipe cleaner handle on back and bend up end into a loop. You can hold her and play this game.

THE HOUSE GAME: The children place their houses in a long row on the table. One child hides a small flat key under one of the houses while the children hide their eyes. Then the children hunt for the key and whoever finds the key can hide it again as game is repeated.

MILK CARTON GRAND-FATHER CLOCK

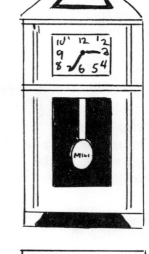

THE CLOCK: Cut out an opening for the pendulum in a half-gallon milk carton. Cut a hole on each side directly opposite each other, right above the open cutout area. Push a pipe cleaner through the two holes. Tape down the two ends to the carton.

TOP OF CLOCK: Cut out, paint and glue on this top for the clock.

PENDULUM: Cut out construction paper oval shape, tape one end of a pipe cleaner on back, then twist the top of pipe cleaner over the other pipe cleaner inside of the clock.

FACE OF CLOCK: Cut a small hole in center of a construction paper square on which clock numbers have been drawn. Cut out black paper hands and attach with paper fastener to face. Paint clock. When dry, glue on clock's face. Use it to play house.

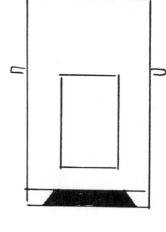

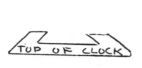

TOP OF CLOCK

BACK VIEW

HANDS

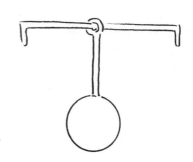

SCARY NOISE MAKER

Drop a few stones into an empty one-quart milk carton. Staple the top closed. Glue colorful crepe paper around the milk carton. Cut a slit on each side, opposite each other. Push a strip of cardboard through one slit and out the other side.

FOR WINGS

WINGS are crepe paper folded over each wing piece, glued on and a fringe cut along the edges. Cut out more FRINGES to glue around body one above the other, starting at the bottom.

FACE AND HORNS: Draw on separate paper. Color and cut them out and glue in place. Glue one more fringe around top of his head. Shake him to the rhythm of music or use him as a NOISE-MAKER.

FRINGE

HORNS

A VARIETY OF PAPER PROJECTS

LITTLE COWBOY

Make card-board pattern of boy and hat brim.

BRIM OF HAT PATTERN

PATTERN

Trace patterns onto white paper. Color and cut out. LEGS: Tape each leg extension back, to form two tubes. PUT ON HIS HAT BRIM by cutting a slit for the crown of hat to go through.

LASSO: Twist string through his armhole. Put two fingers into leg tubes to make him walk.

SEESAW

The children go up and down.

BASE TO HOLD SEESAW BOARD: Cut out a 7½ by 4-inch-high rectangle of construction paper.

3"

1½"

3"

SEESAW (cont'd.):

Fold sections on dotted lines (see preceding page). Fold up the 3-inch sides. Make a hole in the center of the top of each folded up side.

SEESAW BOARD:

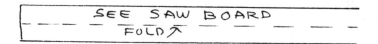

Cut out a rectangle of construction paper 2 by 12 inches long. Fold the 12-inch length in half and glue the two sides together. Place seesaw inside the top part of the BASE. Make a hole on each side of base and push a pipe cleaner through the holes and board and fold over each end. The seesaw can now go up and down. Make a cardboard pattern of two seated children. Trace them onto heavy white paper, color and cut out. STAPLE ON each end of the board.

MOTHER'S DAY FLOWERS

FLOWER POT: Cut a piece of con-
struction paper 12 by 4½ inches in half lengthwise.

THE FLOWERS: The stems are pipe cleaners. Color them green with crayons. THE LEAVES are cut out of green crepe paper and glued onto the stems.

THE FLOWERS are small cutout squares of crepe paper, with the top of each stem folded over   center

FLOWER POT (cont'd.):

of each flower. Make as many as you wish. PUT FLOWER POT TOGETHER: Lay the flower stems along the inside top of the pot. Staple each stem. Staple the two sides of the pot together to form a tube shape. Tape a crepe paper ribbon around the pot to finish it.

FATHER'S DAY PRESENT:
A PLACE TO PUT BILLS

Use one round oatmeal box; don't use the lid. Cut out white paper that will encircle the oatmeal box. Glue it onto the box. Draw on the face with a fine black marker. Print BILLS on his collar. Now he is all ready for father to use as a special holder. Make one for yourself and for your mother with the right face drawn on. It is fun to have things all organized.

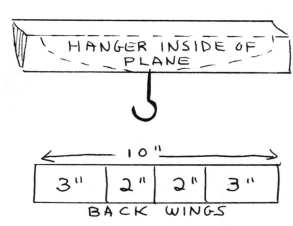

BODY:
Cut out a heavy piece of paper 16 by 11 inches. Fold down the two sides. Plane is 16 inches long and will now be 5 inches wide. The remaining 1 inch width is the top of the plane. Round off the bottom corners with scissors. Draw and color the plane. Place and tape a wire hanger inside the body. The top of hanger is at the bottom as a handle. Glue sides together.

FRONT WINGS: Cut out cardboard wings 16 by 2 inches. Glue on construction paper the same size. Print child's name on the wings. Glue onto top front of plane.

TAIL: Cut out construction paper 10 inches long by 2 inches wide. Fold 10-inch length in half and then fold up

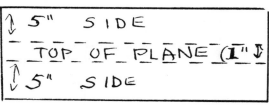

5" SIDE
TOP OF PLANE (1")
5" SIDE

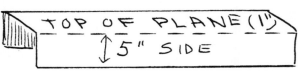

TOP OF PLANE (1")
5" SIDE

HANGER INSIDE OF PLANE

3"	2"	2"	3"

10"

BACK WINGS

each 3-inch end of the tail. Staple or glue the tail onto the airplane. It is now ready to fly.

BODY: Cut out two paper strips, each 1 2 by 1 inch. See picture. Staple A on top of B at a right angle. Fold B over A, then A over B. Continue crisscrossing over each other until the strips become like an accordian. Staple the ends together to complete the body. Head is made by drawing two matching heads and two ears. Glue heads together. Draw EYES, NOSE and MOUTH. Staple on EARS and staple HEAD to BODY. Cut out a bow. Staple on two sets of pipe cleaner legs and a tail and a bow.

GET - WELL CARD FROM US ALL

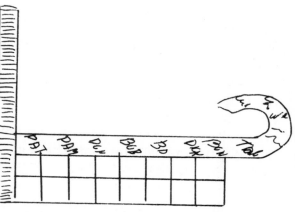

THE BED: One shoe box will become the bed. Turn it upside down and paint it. Also paint the lid. Let it dry. Spread glue on one end of shoe box. Stand up lid and press it inside against the glued area to become the headboard. The BLANKET is decorated paper glued onto top and sides of the box. Then make the MESSAGE PILLOW from a long white sheet of paper that is the width of the top of the bed. The children write get-well messages on it. Glue the top to the top of the bed, by the headboard. Roll it up to look like a pillow and fasten it with a paper clip.

DOUBLE - DECKER BUS

Turn a shoe box upside down. Paint it as a bus. Draw, color and cut out of paper, windows, doors and wheels. Glue them onto the bus. The top of the bus is the lid, glued on, with the inside of lid facing up. Decorate the edges. Draw, color and cut out people. Glue to lid.

(PEOPLE)

Paint a shoe box and its lid bright colors. Let dry. Draw, color and cut out paper windows, doors and wheels. Glue them on. Cut the doors so they can open. TROLLEY: Make a small hole in lid; tape one end of a pipe cleaner inside. The rest is bent into a trolley. Put the lid back in place. PEOPLE: Draw, color and cut out paper people and tape a piece of pipe cleaner on back as a handle.

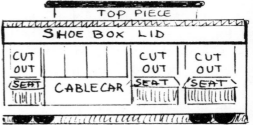

CABLE CAR

Paint shoe-box car and its lid roof. Draw top piece of cable car on construction paper. Fold it in half; then fold up bottom pieces, as tabs to glue onto roof, after you color and cut it out. Draw, color, cut out and glue on windows, doors, wheels, etc. PAPER PEOPLE: Draw, color and cut out. Tape pipe cleaner handles on back.

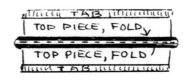

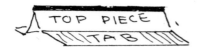

FIRST PUPPET, A WHAT-NOTITY

This puppet can talk and sing to you. His HEAD is a 9-inch-tall tube from a 9 by 12-inch piece of construction paper. Staple ends together. Cut an oval opening for the beak in front. The BEAK is made from a 5 by 9-inch piece of orange construction paper. Roll it into a narrow 9-inch tube. Glue the edges together. Then in the center of this tube, cut an oval 1 by 2-inches long. Fold this tube in half, as the BEAK. The cutout oval is on the outside top and bottom of the BEAK. Place this BEAK fold into the open oval of the HEAD. Put transparent tape across the inside of the BEAK and onto the HEAD on both sides. Your thumb and finger enter the BEAK from inside the head.

FEATHERS: Cut out two 9 by 12-inch pieces of crepe paper. Cut a fringe along the 12-inch edges as feathers. Glue them double thickness around the head of the puppet, starting by one side of the beak and going around the head to other side of beak.

PAPER PUPPET CREATURES (cont'd.):

EYES: Draw with black fine line marker on white paper, cut out and glue onto head.

TOPKNOT: Cut a fringe on top side of a square piece of crepe paper. Staple on top of head. Put your hand inside and with thumb and finger in two holes of beak to move it, sing this song:

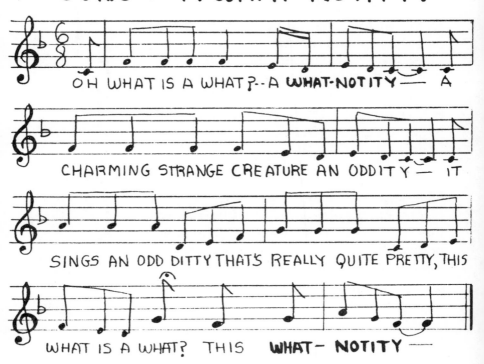

The children learn the song, and all of the WHAT-NOTITY puppets they make sing the song as a chorus of the WHAT-NOTITY puppets sing happily together.

SECOND PUPPET, A TWITTER BIRD

THE HEAD: Staple two small paper plates together around the edges. The backs of the plates face out. Cut a vertical oval through the center of both plates, large enough for your thumb and finger to enter the back and come out the front. Draw two EYES with black fine marker. Cut out a crepe paper square; cut fringe on top. Staple on top of HEAD.

BODY: Cut off the closed top of a cereal box, then cut down the two side panels of box, about 3 inches. Fold them out to become WINGS. Cover wings by glueing on many strips of crepe paper with fringe cut along one edge of each piece. Also cover BODY with crepe paper fringes. SHOES: Cut out construction paper ovals and glue on bottom with feet sticking out. Operate the bird by wearing a colored glove and long sleeved T-shirt which becomes the neck and beak. Put

TWITTER BIRD (cont'd.):

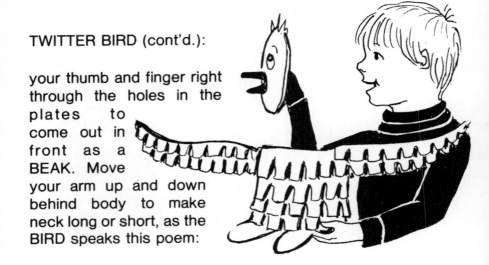

your thumb and finger right through the holes in the plates to come out in front as a BEAK. Move your arm up and down behind body to make neck long or short, as the BIRD speaks this poem:

> I wonder if you ever heard
> That I'm a twitty, TWITTER BIRD;
> It's funny fun, it's quite absurd;
> Don't speak, just twitter every word.

BIRD and audience can TWITTER to the music of a record. Children love the funny twitter sounds they make.

THIRD PUPPET, NELL GAZELLE

BODY is a 9-inch square piece of construction paper. Fold in half. Round off the bottom corners with scissors. The fold becomes the back of NELL GAZELLE.

LEGS AND NECK: Each piece is a tube, formed from a piece of construction paper 7 inches long by 4 inches wide. Roll each piece into a long 7-inch tube. Tape around the tops and bottoms with cellophane tape.

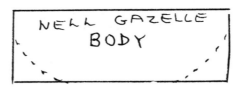

NELL GAZELLE, PUPPET (cont'd.): Cut a slit on the front top of the BODY for the NECK to slip into. Staple it in place. Glue a black crepe paper fringe on the neck. Staple the top part of each leg onto inside edge of the BODY. HEAD: Fold a 9 by 2½-inch rectangle in half; the folded part in back of head is glued around top of neck. Decorate with markers. Cut out and glue on two EARS; staple on a TAIL. One finger in a back leg and one in a front leg holds the puppet.

POEM

Oh let me tell of Nell Gazelle,
That's ME, a graceful island belle;
I leap and soar and proudly prance
Behold this Nell Gazelle must DANCE!

Record plays as Nell dances and audience claps to the rhythmic beat of the happy recording. She can dance on the edge of a table or above a bookcase with the puppeteer reaching up from below. SEE *GOOD APPLE PUPPET BOOK* FOR MORE IDEAS.

TRAPEZE ARTISTS

Make a cardboard pattern of these TRAPEZE ARTISTS. Trace around the pattern onto white cardboard. Color on both sides and cut out. Punch a hole in each leg where the bar goes through.

TRAPEZE: Shape two triangles from two long pipe cleaners. Push them through the legholes. Then fasten ends by twisting them. Tie the tops of each trapeze to a stick with yarn. Now holding the stick with one hand, push the trapeze artists and watch them swing back and forth.

PLAYMATE (MADE FROM NEWSPAPER)

BODY: Open up one colored comic sheet from a small size paper. Fold lengthwise, into 3 long parts. Then fold the whole folded paper in half. The fold is the bottom of body.

PLAYMATE (cont'd.):

HEAD: Staple two paper plates together around the top and side rims. Leave bottom open. Backs of plates show. Draw and color face; glue on crepe paper hair. The two end pieces of body are pushed into the opening at bottom of head. Staple in place. The folded part of body remains at the bottom.

ARMS: Roll up a sheet of newspaper. Push it through the front and back space of the folded body. Cut off excess end pieces. Staple arms in place and tie a ribbon around the waist. LEGS: Roll up a sheet of newspaper. Staple the ends. Push it through open body space above the fold. Fold down the legs and staple where needed. SKIRT: Cut a long rectangle of crepe paper and glue top of skirt, under ribbon and around her waist.

NEWSPAPER CREATURE

Roll a small size newspaper sheet as BODY. Glue edges. LEGS: Roll two newspaper sheets into two long tubes as four legs. Glue over front and back of body. HEAD and NECK are one piece of newspaper rolled into

NEWSPAPER CREATURE (cont'd.):

a long tube shape. Glue the edges. Put one end inside the rolled body tube. Glue or staple it in place, so that the neck is in a vertical position. Fold over the top of neck to become the head.

Staple it in this position a little beyond the fold, so the fold can look like two ears. Paint on eyes, nose and mouth. Glue on a crepe paper mane by cutting one edge as a fringe. Cut out a crepe paper tail and glue on back.

CARDBOARD TUBES

A LAMB

BODY: Use one empty toilet tissue tube. Make four holes with a paper punch, one for each leg to come through. LEGS: Color two pipe cleaners with black crayon. Push one pipe cleaner through the front two legholes. Fold down each end, then fold up the ends to give double thickness to the legs. Make the back two legs the same way. NECK and TAIL are another pipe cleaner taped inside the top of the tube. One end comes out the front as the NECK. The

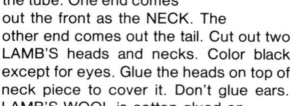

other end comes out the tail. Cut out two LAMB'S heads and necks. Color black except for eyes. Glue the heads on top of neck piece to cover it. Don't glue ears. LAMB'S WOOL is cotton glued on.

TUBE PEOPLE, A HOUSE AND A PALM TREE

HEAD: Using heavy white paper, draw, color and cut out a paper head with a tab at the bottom. Glue the tab part to inside top of toilet tissue tube. Punch two armholes in the tube with a paper

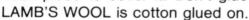

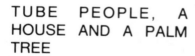

TUBE PEOPLE (cont'd.):

punch. Push a long pipe cleaner through the two holes. Fold over the ends as arms (double thickness). Cut a space between the legs. Paint clothes.

A HOUSE TO LIVE IN: Cover a cereal box with paper. Draw the windows, door and roof with marker. Cut out back of house for people to play inside. PALM TREE: Use a longer tube. Paint it brown. Cut a few slits at the bottom to spread out and staple to the backside of a paper plate. Paint plate green. TREETOP: Glue the ends of green crepe paper leaves inside open top of tube with the leaves extending outside.

CONSTRUCTION PAPER ANIMALS

ELEPHANT

Cut out a piece of construction paper 4½ by 9

ELEPHANT (cont'd.):

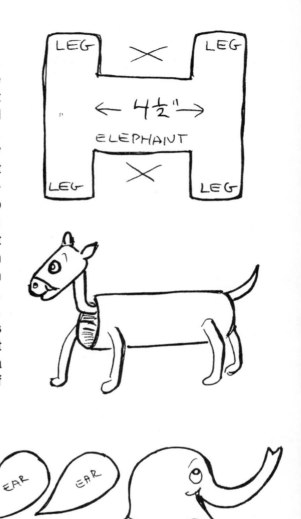

inches to become the BODY and LEGS. Cut out the spaces marked X between the legs. Glue the cutout body onto an empty toilet tissue tube so legs extend below to hold up the BODY. HEAD: Draw an elephant head, neck and tab on matching construction paper. Make TWO. Draw eyes and mouth. Glue head pieces together and cut out and glue on ears. Cut a slit on top front of BODY. Glue tabs of neck inside tube of body. Make MORE this way and have your own paper ZOO.

TUBE ANIMAL

BODY is a painted toilet tissue tube. Punch four holes where the legs go. Push a pipe cleaner through the front two holes and bend down the two legs, then fold them up for a double thickness. Fold up toes. Make the back two legs the same way. HEAD AND TAIL: Tape a pipe cleaner inside top of

TUBE ANIMAL (cont'd.):

tube. One end of pipe cleaner comes out the front as a NECK. The other end comes out the back as a TAIL. Draw, color and cut out two identical heads. Glue together, covering the neck piece.

"ME" AND MY SWING

On 9 by 12-inch pink construction paper, draw, color and cut out top part of child minus the arms. Fold up end of the shirt. Cut out of construction paper 12-inch-long arms. Glue arms behind body with arms coming out on each side.

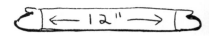

LEGS are colored and cut out of construction paper; each is glued under edge of skirt. Fold up the feet. THE SWING: Run a string of yarn through an empty tube so that 16 inches extends out and up to tie each end to the bottom bar of a wire clothes hanger. Glue folded up skirt onto SEAT OF SWING. Fold each hand over the yarn pieces of swing. Glue them closed.

BOY ON SWING has different clothes, but is made the same way as the girl is made. Paint them.

A GNOME

HEAD AND BODY: Use an empty toilet tissue cardboard tube. Mark off the top area for the head. Paint it flesh color. Paint on the eyes, nose and mouth. Paint the body any color that you like. Also paint on the belt and a buckle. ARMS: Cut out one piece, about 4 inches long. Paint the sleeves . Cut a slit on each side of the body to push the arms through so one arm and hand come out of each side. WHISKERS: Glue on cotton whiskers and a small mustache. HIS HAT: Cut out a red crepe paper rectangle 6 by 5 inches. Glue the 6-inch edge around top of head and staple top into a point. FEET: Cut out two construction paper ovals. Turn up one end of each oval to glue to inside of the tube. The remaining parts come out in front as the shoes. You can make a family of gnomes, tube forest trees and cereal box houses for a village of gnomes. (See TUBE PEOPLE page 66.) Act out little fairy tales with everyone creating his own and playing together.

CONSTRUCTION PAPER

GROUP PROJECTS, TABLE PLAY

TABLE PLAY

THE CITY PLAYBOARD

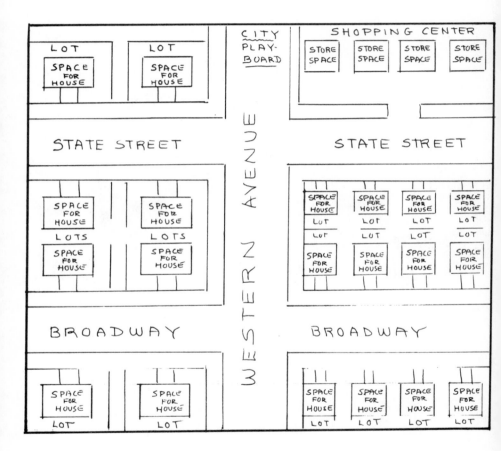

The directions for making this board are on the next page.

TABLE PLAY (cont'd.):

The CITY PLAYBOARD can be made on a large poster-like board, using the white side of the board. Draw CITY STREETS, LOTS AND SIDEWALKS of your own creation. (See sample illustration.) Use markers or crayons, or paint with acrylic paint. The board can be covered with heavy clear acetate to protect it. The city can be drawn on unbleached sheeting with colored crayons that can be ironed for permanence. Sew elastic at each corner to fit over a long table.

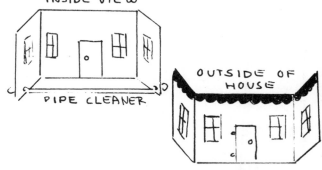

INSIDE VIEW

OUTSIDE OF HOUSE

PIPE CLEANER

HOUSES AND STORES

Each child makes his own house out of stiff paper, folded into three sections: the front of the house and its two sides. Draw on the windows and doors. When finished, punch a hole at the bottom end of each side. Push a piece of pipe cleaner through the two holes to hold the house together in the back. Stores are made the same way. Set the house or store on one of the empty lots on the playboard.

PEOPLE

PEOPLE: On heavy white paper, draw and color a family of paper people to

BACK

live inside of the house or to work in the store. Cut them out and tape a piece of pipe cleaner on back of each, to use as a handle to move them about or for them to stand alone.

SLIP ON CAR: Fold a piece of construction
paper in half. Cut an opening on the FOLD
to slip on over the paper person's head, and this little person
has his own car to ride around in. Draw the car wheels and
doors.

A COUNTRY PLAYBOARD

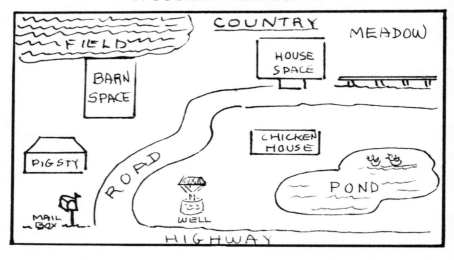

Draw and paint on the white side of a large poster-like board
the parts of a farm that you would like represented, such as
the HOUSE area, BARN, a FIELD, PIGPEN, CHICKEN
COOP, WELL, MEADOW, POND, etc. Then make the
FARMHOUSE, BARN, etc., the same way that you made
the city houses and stores.

PAPER PEOPLE AND ANIMALS: Make them like you made
the paper CITY PEOPLE.

SEASHORE PLAYBOARD

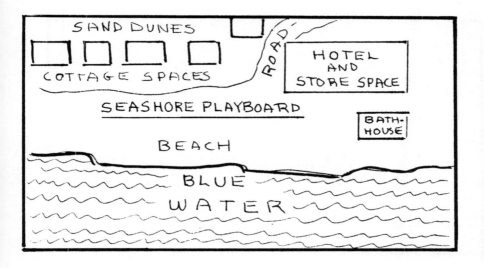

Construct a **SEASHORE PLAYBOARD** as illustrated. COTTAGE and HOTEL (with a combination of a store, restaurant, post office and boat rental service) can be made like the CITY HOUSE (with three sides).

BOATS can be three sided, too, a bottom and two sides of construction paper folded up.

WILD WEST PLAYBOARD

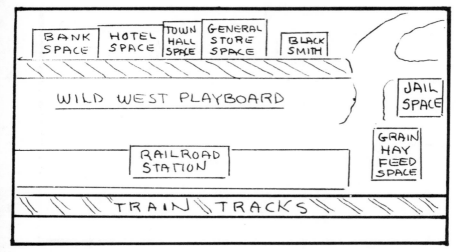

Create your own WILD WEST PLAYBOARD like the wild west you see on television and in movies. Make an old town of three-sided buildings. (See the CITY BUILDING SECTION.) Also refer to this section for making the people (cowboys) and horses. Make a three-sided TRAIN, with a bottom and two sides folded up. All are made of paper.

WORLD MAP PLAYBOARD

Mount a world map on cardboard. Cover it with heavy clear acetate. Children learn places, customs, products, etc., as they play with toy boats, planes, and trains. They travel all over the world.

GAMES TO MAKE AND PLAY

WISHING GAME

TWO CHILDREN WILL NEED: (1) A MAGIC CIRCLE cut out of cardboard to sit on.
(2) A MAGIC WAND. Use a stick.
(3) 25 WISHING CARDS. Use 25 small index cards.

LET'S MAKE THE 25 WISHING CARDS (includes 5 loss cards).

    (1) A GOLDEN CROWN worth 2 million dollars.
    (2) A CASTLE worth 10 million dollars.
    (3) CROWN JEWELS worth 5 million dollars.
    (4) A SMALL VILLAGE worth 3 million dollars.
    (5) A ROYAL YACHT worth 2 million dollars.
    (6) A BANK ACCOUNT worth 10 million dollars.
    (7) A VACATION ISLAND worth 5 million dollars.
    (8) A PRIVATE ZOO worth 2 million dollars.
    (9) A TOY FACTORY worth 1 million dollars.

WISHING GAME (cont'd.):

(10) A PRIVATE RIVER WITH BOATS worth 3 million dollars.

(11) (LOSS CARD) Your opponent steals one of your cards.

(12) (LOSS CARD) You donate a card to charity.

(13) (LOSS CARD) You are in debt; forfeit a card.

(14) (LOSS CARD) You didn't pay taxes; give a card to the government.

(15) (LOSS CARD) A big storm takes everything, so put back ALL of your cards.

(16) OCEAN LINER IS YOURS, worth 3 million dollars.

(17) YOU INHERIT A BUBBLE GUM FACTORY worth 1 million dollars.

(18) SOMEONE LEFT YOU A CANDY FACTORY worth 1 million dollars.

(19) YOU INHERIT A HOTEL worth 2 million dollars.

(20) A SHOPPING CENTER IS YOURS worth 3 million dollars.

(21) YOU NOW OWN A SPACESHIP worth 5 million dollars.

(22) YOUR UNCLE JUST LEFT YOU A MOUNTAIN worth 2 million dollars.

(23) YOU INHERIT A GOLD MINE worth 3 million dollars.

(24) YOU JUST WON AN AMUSEMENT PARK worth 3 million dollars.

(25) YOU INHERITED YOUR FATHER'S UNIVERSITY worth 5 million dollars.

HOW TO PLAY THE GAME: Spread all of the cards, face down on the floor. Two children take alternating turns, ten turns each. The first child sits on the MAGIC CIRCLE holding a MAGIC WAND. The child spins around once in a sitting position on the MAGIC CIRCLE. He immediately touches a

WISHING GAME (cont'd.):
card and does what the card says, if it is a LOSS CARD. He reads his card aloud. The GAME continues until the two children have each picked up their ten cards. Add up score to see who wins, or play until all cards are used.

A SNAIL GAME

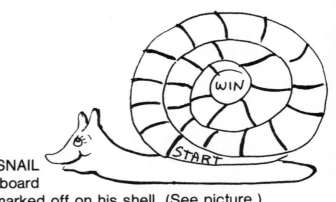

Draw a large SNAIL on white cardboard with sections marked off on his shell. (See picture.)

TWO CHILDREN PLAY THIS GAME: A STONE is tossed in this game. Paint no. 1 on one side of the stone and no. 2 on the other side. Each child places his own BUTTON on START. Each child takes a turn tossing the STONE up. When it lands, he moves his BUTTON one space if the STONE'S number is 1, two spaces if it shows a 2. Take turns until one child reaches the center of the SNAIL SHELL.

COWBOY ROUNDUP GAME

Each child wears a crepe paper horse's tail.

Choose two TEAMS. One team is the WILD HORSE TEAM; the other TEAM is the TAME HORSE TEAM.

HOW TO PLAY THE GAME: Both TEAMS are behind a make-believe fence. All of the children pretend to be HORSES. The children, as HORSES, must play the game bending over with their hands touching the ground. The teacher blows a whistle and the TAME HORSE TEAM tries to capture as many of the WILD HORSE TEAM as they can by tagging them before they reach a designated area of freedom called THE WIDE OPEN SPACES. Any horse that reaches THE WIDE OPEN SPACES without being tagged is FREE and cannot be captured. Count up the WILD HORSES captured. Then repeat the game with the WILD HORSES trying to capture the TAME HORSES. Count the score for TAME HORSES captured to see which TEAM WINS!

HAND GOLF FOR CHILDREN

TAKE NINE DOWEL STICKS. Glue the end of a numbered flag on the top end of each stick. Number the flags from 1 to 9. Twist a large pipe cleaner to form a circle and fasten to the bottom of a stick to represent the HOLE for the BALL to enter. Do this to each of the nine sticks. Place the nine flags with their sticks around the playground, some distance apart. Push each stick firmly into the ground. The pipe cleaner circle at the bottom of each stick rests on the ground.

HOW TO PLAY THE GAME: Each child alternates, hitting his own colored ball, one HIT with his hand for each turn. The children must reach hole one, continue on to hole two, etc., until one child has entered all nine holes BEFORE his opponent. This child is the WINNER!

HAUNTED HOUSE GAME

Two children play. Decorate a cardboard carton to look like a HAUNTED HOUSE. Cut out the windows and door spaces. Number the windows 5 and 10 and the door space 15. Now let's PLAY THE GAME: Two children want to scare the ghost out of the haunted house. Each child has a STONE. He/She takes 10 alternate turns tossing the stone. Each child adds up his score for each WINDOW and DOOR the stone goes through. The child with the highest score wins!

SPACE FLIGHT

Gather fifty STONES. Paint some with a RED spot, some with a blue spot, some with a YELLOW spot. Each RED stone is worth 5 dollars, and each YELLOW stone is worth 20 dollars.

SPACE FLIGHT (cont'd.):

NOW BEGIN THE GAME: The teacher hides the stones all over the playground, pretending it is another planet the children will land on, to hunt for rare stones to bring back to Earth. The teacher calls, then all the children fly around the planet playground to gather colored stone samples in their lunch bags they used at lunchtime. About ten minutes later, the teacher blows her whistle, calls again and the children fly back to Earth inside the classroom with their colored stones. Each sack is counted for its value. The child with the highest score WINS!

BUILD A MALL GAME

(Two children play.) Each child must pile up 10 blocks to make one STORE. Make a sign with name of mall. The teacher blows a whistle. The first child to complete his MALL of 5 STORES and stand up his sign wins!

BUILD A HOUSE GAME

Two children play. Each child draws, colors and cuts out a cardboard roof that can fit the top of his house which will have 4 walls and be 5 blocks high. The children compete to be first to complete a house. If a block is dropped, just pick it up and keep on building. (DON'T START OVER.)

SKYSCRAPER   GAME

Tape a large rectangle of paper on the wall to be the SKYSCRAPER APARTMENT BUILDING. The children draw and cut out many windows from a cardboard pattern. Tape only the tops of the windows onto the SKYSCRAPER. Draw and cut out the top of a man, smaller than the windows so he cannot be seen hiding in back

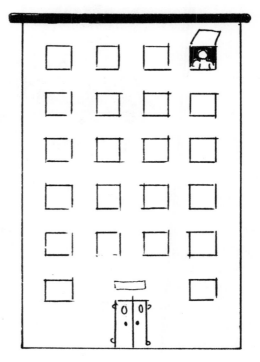

85

SKYSCRAPER GAME (cont'd.):

of one of the windows. (The teacher tapes him there while the children hide their eyes.) Then the children are invited, one at a time, to guess where the man is hiding. The first child to guess where he is, wins a chance to hide the man in a different place to repeat the game. Continue to play. Try this also with two teams competing and alternating turns guessing.

OCEAN LINER OR CRUISE SHIP GAME

BOAT: Draw, paint, cut out a cardboard SHIP. Staple two cloth tape loops on back, one for each child to carry his end of the boat.

LET'S PLAY THIS GEOGRAPHY-TYPE QUIZ GAME

Choose one child to start the game. This child chooses a partner. The children carry the BOAT.   They whisper to the teacher which COUNTRY they plan to use for the quiz. The children then sail, (walk) into the room carrying their BOAT in front of them speaking the SWISH, SWISH, SWISH poem on the next page.

OCEAN LINER OR CRUISE SHIP GAME (cont'd.):
POEM:
SWISH, SWISH, SWISH.
The waves took us back, we're back home to stay.
SWISH, SWISH, SWISH!
Now where have we been? What do you say?

The children try to guess which country the SHIP CHILDREN visited as hints are given to the children guessing until someone guesses correctly to win a trip. Repeat the game.

STORE AND RESTAURANT GAMES

STORE GAME

Cut out familiar grocery products from magazines. Put them into a paper bag.

One child is the SHOPPER, who holds the bag. The SHOPPER reaches into bag, takes one item and peeks inside to see what she has chosen. (The others must not see the items.) They keep guessing until some child guesses the correct item. Give hints if it is necessary. The child who guesses the item is now the SHOPPER as the game is repeated as often as you wish.

RESTAURANT GAME

The teacher makes up a simple restaurant menu with prices, a la carte items, etc. She reads the menu aloud but not the prices. In this game the children compete to spend the LEAST AMOUNT of money for a COMPLETE MEAL. The teacher takes each child's order on separate checks. The child with the lowest price on his check WINS. NOTE: In preparation for this game, copy menus and prices from restaurants, including fast food places. This game teaches children how to save money, then perhaps they can eat out more often with the money left over.

EXTRA FUN AND PLAY: The children can also design their own restaurant menus with prices. Cut food pictures out of magazines or draw, color and cut them out. Pretend to run your own restaurant--plan costs, serve on paper plates, etc.

VALENTINE PARTY

Each child decorates a heart. The teacher collects the hearts. The teacher numbers ALL of the HEARTS IN PAIRS. Each heart has its matching number. Example: Two HEARTS are numbered 1, two HEARTS are numbered 2, and so on. Until each HEART has an identical number on the back of one other HEART. If there is an UNEVEN number of children, make a leftover heart with its back blank. The child who gets this heart becomes the HOST or HOSTESS for the party. All of the HEARTS are placed in a VALENTINE BOX. Each child draws out ONE HEART and looks on the back to see the NUMBER. Then he walks about trying to find WHO has the same number he has to become his partner for the party.

A HEART GAME

One blank paper heart folded in half is given to children. One child draws an eye, half of a nose and half of a mouth on HIS HALF side of the HEART. The child must not look to see what the other partner has drawn. The partner now draws on the blank side his created eye, half of a nose and half of a mouth. Then the HEARTS are opened and held up for all to enjoy.

TIME TO SERVE PARTY FOOD

SUGGESTION: Pink lemonade and heart-shaped cookies. Then play HIDE THE HEART GAME. One child leaves the room. The other children sit or stand in a circle. The teacher gives a child a small paper HEART to hold in his closed hand. All of the children close their hands pretending to hold the HEART but keeping it a SECRET. The child who left the room now returns to guess which child is holding the HEART. The children hum softly and as the child gets closer to the hidden HEART, they hum louder until the HEART is found. Repeat game as often as you like.

SAINT PATRICK'S DAY PARTY

START WITH A DANCE: Let's get into the spirit of Saint Patrick's Day and dance to happy Irish music. Put on a record. Everyone DANCE! Then play FIND THE SHAMROCK game. Draw, color and cut out a LEPRECHAUN'S HAT and tape it on the wall. Cut out about 25 different sized green shamrocks. Also cut out two identically shaped shamrocks and tape one on the hat. Hide ALL of the other shamrocks by taping them all around the room, while the children hide their eyes. When the teacher blows a whistle, the children hunt for the shamrocks.

SAINT PATRICK'S DAY PARTY (cont'd.):

They hold on to every one they find. When they are all found, each child steps up to the HAT on the wall and holds up each of his shamrocks to the shamrock on the HAT to see if one of his shamrocks is the exact match of the HAT shamrock. All the children have a turn. The WINNER is the child who holds the matching HAT shamrock.

SUGGESTIONS FOR REFRESHMENT TIME: Serve limeade and cake with a green frosting or frosted shamrock on it. After eating let's play another game. FOLLOW THE LEPRECHAUN game. The children all pretend that they are leprechauns. They move about the room in different positions that the teacher calls out, such as JUMP, CRAWL, HOP, TWIRL, MARCH, TAKE TINY STEPS, etc. Whoever does not immediately follow the teacher's directions has to sit down and watch. The winner is the last child to leave the game--the smartest leprechaun.

EASTER PARTY

A BUNNY TAIL GAME: The children begin by cutting out two white paper BUNNY EARS. Half of the children staple their ears onto a blue headband; the other half staple their ears onto a green headband. All the children put on their

A BUNNY TAIL GAME (cont'd.):

headbands. The BLUE head-bands represent one team and the GREEN headbands represent the other team. The green head-band children are given green paper BUNNY TAILS and the blue headband children are given blue paper BUNNY TAILS.

PLAY THE GAME: Each child holds his BUNNY TAIL behind him with one hand and must try to take as many BUNNY TAILS of his opposite team as he can while protecting his own tail from being snatched. As soon as any child has his own tail taken from him, he must leave the game and watch. Continue until all tails are taken. Count up tails taken by both teams. The team with the most captured tails, WINS! Any-time bunny ears fall off during game they must be put back in place, then the child can continue to play.

SUGGESTIONS FOR PARTY REFRESHMENTS: Pastel colored milk shakes, pastel frosted cupcakes with a few jelly beans on top to look like Easter eggs.

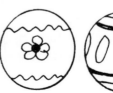

EASTER EGG FUN

MAKE AN EASTER EGG: Everyone draws a pretty decorated Easter egg on paper and cuts it out. On the back of each egg, he writes down a simple, funny stunt to perform. All eggs are collected and taped onto the wall for an exhibition. The children vote for the prettiest egg. A BLUE RIBBON is given to the winner. (Don't put ribbon on the wall.)

The children sit in a row facing the Easter eggs. One child steps up, chooses an egg (NOT HIS OWN), and reads the stunt he must perform written on the back. The child performs the stunt then returns the egg to the child who made it, to take home. This child now chooses an egg to repeat the action, etc., until all have had turns.

HALLOWEEN PARTY

Make a large paper haunted house around a door. This real door becomes the door of the haunted house. Let's start the party with a game.

THE HAUNTED HOUSE SCARES ME GAME

Divide the group into two teams, a BOYS' TEAM and a GIRLS' TEAM.

THE HAUNTED HOUSE SCARES ME GAME (cont'd.):

The GIRLS' TEAM stays in the darkened room. The BOYS' TEAM goes out the haunted door to wait to be called. The teacher tells each girl what type of spooky sound she should make.

EXAMPLES: HOOT like an OWL. MEOW like a scared CAT. HOWL like the WIND. STAMP FEET like an angry GOBLIN. CACKLE like a WITCH. LAUGH like a MONSTER. ROAR like a GIANT. SAY WHOOO like a GHOST or any other scary sound that you can create. The BOYS come back into the HAUNTED ROOM and walk slowly through as the GIRLS try to scare them with their spooky sounds. Everyone has a good time. Now repeat the fun with the GIRLS going outside, then returning to the room that is darkened and the BOYS try to scare the GIRLS.

THE PUMPKIN GAME

Make a paper pumpkin, color it and cut it out. Draw and color a pumpkin on a paper bag to fit over a child's head.

PUMPKIN GAME (cont'd.):

Choose one child to wear the paper bag over his head, so he can't see. The remaining children form a circle around him. Give one of the children the paper pumpkin to hold. The child with the paper bag over his head must find the paper pumpkin. As he gets close to the paper pumpkin the children all say, "Ooooooooh." Continue until the PUMPKIN is found.

PARTY FOOD SUGGESTIONS: Serve apple cider with open-face pimento cheese spread on round bread slices, decorated with faces made with black olive pieces.

TRICK OR TREAT! WHAT'S IN THE BAG ?

Cut out numerous cardboard shapes of familiar objects-animals, etc. Place one or two in each of the lunch-size paper bags which are clipped onto a clothesline. One child at a time reaches into each bag to try to recognize the shape and identify what is inside without looking. Then the child whispers to the teacher what he thinks is inside the bag. The teacher writes down how many he identified correctly. Each child does this. After each child has had his turn, the scores are compared to see who WINS!

NOTE: When not playing the game, the cardboard shapes can be used as PATTERNS to trace and draw at a coloring table.

GIFT GAME: Two teams play this game. Everyone draws a gift with a ribbon on a piece of paper. Each child donates one picture gift to the teacher. She shows all the gifts to the children. Then she staples one gift picture on the back of each gift package she collected from the children. No child sees which picture she puts on back of any package. The gifts are all put into a shopping bag. NOW LET'S PLAY THE GAME: Choose two teams. The teacher shows one gift at a time, showing only the ribbon side of the package, as the children try to guess what is on the other side. Whoever guesses correctly keeps the gift on his team. Continue holding up gifts until all are guessed. The team with the most gifts win.

WHO AM I?

Draw score papers. The GIRLS compete against the BOYS. The teacher whispers to a girl chosen to start the game; she is told what toy she is supposed to be. The girl acts out the part of the TOY, until one of the teams guesses what TOY she is supposed to be. The one who guesses wins a point for his or her team and now is told by the teacher what TOY to act out, as before. Continue for a preplanned amount of time. The WINNER is the team which has the most points.

TIME FOR CHRISTMAS REFRESHMENTS: You could serve homemade cookies, baked at home or at school, cranberry juice, and little colored candies in a clear plastic bag tied up with a ribbon.

TREE TRIMMING FUN

Make a cardboard shape of a Christmas tree ball. Trace ball onto heavy white paper, then draw a self-portrait in the center. Hang it on your tree.

YOUR LETTER ON THE TREE

Make cardboard patterns of letters of the alphabet. Have each child trace the first letter of his name on paper. Color and cut it out and hang it on your tree. Make letters for other family names to add to the tree trimming.

FOIL BALLS AS A GARLAND

The children can loosely form small balls of silver foil. Thread red or green yarn through a NEEDLE with large eye. Push the needle through a ball and then through a colored bead or colored crepe paper pieces. Continue this until you complete a garland the length that you choose.

MERRY CHRISTMAS....HAPPY HOLIDAYS

WALL AND SKY PROJECTS

FLOWER TAPESTRY

Draw a cardboard pattern of a large flower and a medium-sized flower. Each child traces around one of the flowers onto a large piece of heavy white paper. The children decorate their own flowers with crayons. Fill the paper with flowers. A couple of children take green crayons and draw vines and leaves, joining all of the flowers for a look of continuity. Staple the top of the tapestry. Tie a cord from end to end, to hang it up. This tapestry can also be made on unbleached sheeting. After completing crayon work, iron coloring to give it permanence. The tapestry can be used to decorate the school wall.

A "ME" TAPESTRY

Make these cardboard patterns of a boy and a girl.

PATTERNS

A "ME" TAPESTRY (cont'd.):

The children trace around and color a picture of themselves on a large piece of paper. Read the directions for the FLOWER TAPESTRY. Instead of vines and leaves to fill

in empty spaces, draw colorful balloons with strings.

A FOREST OF PERSONALITY TREES

Each child is given a large piece of white paper to lay on the floor. Draw a tree with a funny personality to be placed in a forest of other funny trees, painted bright green. Leave the whites of the EYES showing, the centers black and the trunk and branches brown. Also have the children paint a strip of paper green, as a ground area where the trees stand. Tack or tape up all the trees on the wall.

SKY PROJECT

Half of the ceiling will be DAYTIME; the other half can be NIGHTTIME. The children make their own clouds and stars with personalities. Someone makes a paper moon and sun. All of the paper clouds, stars, sun and moon are cut out and taped onto the ceiling. Children have fun looking on the ceiling for pictures. On the wall can be back views the children make of themselves, colored and cut out of paper and taped on the wall. A few of the children can make a large paper rainbow and tape it on the wall with the paper children. See illustration.

FISH WITH CREPE PAPER TAILS

PATTERNS: Draw cardboard patterns of two FISH, a fat fish and a thin fish. Each child traces around one of the fish or designs his own freestyle fish on lightweight paper. Decorate the fish with crayons. Cut out.

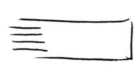

FISH TAIL: Cut out a rectangle of crepe paper with fringe on one end. Staple this tail onto the end of the fish. Tape the fish in the windows to appear as a beautiful transparent water scene with the light shining through the fish as they colorfully swim across the windows to delight the children.

BIRDS AND FLOWERS

BIRDS: Draw these cardboard patterns of a bird flying and a BIRD standing. Each child traces around one BIRD with pencil onto lightweight white paper. Color the BIRDS. Then cut out all

of the birds--tape them in the windows.

PATTERNS

THE FLOWERS: Make the cardboard patterns of these flowers. The children trace around a flower on lightweight white paper, using a pencil. Each child colors his flower with a stem and leaves added, then cuts it out. Tape the birds and flowers onto your windows with cellophane tape, to welcome SPRING. The sunlight shines colorfully through.

BIG BUTTERFLIES

WINGS: Make the wings like picture frames (the centers are cut out). Draw this half wing on cardboard to become a wing pattern. Each child traces around this wing twice on construction paper. Cut out. Turn over one wing to make a pair.

PATTERN

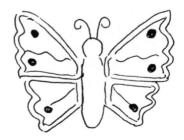

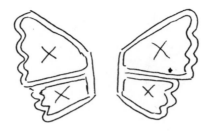

WING FRAMES: Draw the inside shape of the WING FRAME by closely copying its outside shape with a pencil. Cut out the X marked center pieces and the open frame remains. Make two WING FRAMES. Glue colorful crepe paper pieces, colored tissue paper or colored cellophane inside the open X areas. Glue the colored pieces to the frames. Decorate the transparent wings with black marker-type pens.

THE BODY: Make this cardboard pattern to trace onto construction paper. The body can stay opaque or it can also be cut out as a FRAME, like the wings, and have transparent paper glued inside. Use fine wire shaped into feelers and tape to the head. Staple the wings to the body. For a beautiful display of transparent colors, tape the BUTTERFLIES all over the windows. The children can hang them up at home when they no longer decorate the school.

COLORFUL HEART SHAPES FOR THE WINDOW

CRAYON DESIGN HEARTS

Make cardboard patterns of a large and a medium - sized heart. Each child traces around one of the hearts with a pencil or draws his own freestyle heart onto white paper. Decorate the hearts with colorful crayon designs. Cut them out and tape them up in the windows for the light to shine through.

TRANSPARENT FRAME HEARTS

See instructions for making BUTTER-FLY FRAMES (page 106). Use the frames to glue in transparent colorful crepe papers, colored tissue papers or colored cellophane pieces. Draw on black marker designs. Tape the hearts in the windows for the light to shine through the beautiful colors.

FUNNY FACE WINDOW HEARTS

The children draw funny free-heart shapes on lightweight solid colored paper. Cut out the hearts. This is a good

FUNNY FACE WINDOW HEARTS (cont'd.):

scissors project. Draw a funny face with the eye areas cut out except for the black eyespots. All are drawn with a black marker. Also draw and cut out the mouth parts. Tape these hearts on the windows. The light not only shines through the colored hearts but also comes through the cutout eyes, nose and mouth of each heart.

WE SEE YOU

Each child draws a self-portrait on lightweight paper and colors it. Tape the cutout pictures in the windows with the drawing against the window. Now those who pass by on the outside can see all of the children's pictures looking at them. The light shines through and the children can also see themselves from the INSIDE of the room. Each child can improve the inside view by going up to his picture and carefully tracing around all of the lines of his picture with a fine line black marker. This will emphasize the picture to show up more clearly in the room.